50 Things to Know

50 THINGS TO KNOW WHEN BECOMING SUCCESSFUL

INSIGHTS TO REACHING
AND BEING YOUR BEST

MERYLEE SEVILLA

50 Things to Know When Becoming Successful Copyright © 2018 by CZYK Publishing LLC. All Rights Reserved.

All rights reserved. No part of this book may be reproduced in any form or by any electronic or mechanical means including information storage and retrieval systems, without permission in writing from the author. The only exception is by a reviewer, who may quote short excerpts in a review.

The statements in this book are of the authors and may not be the views of CZYK Publishing or 50 Things to Know.

Cover designed by: Ivana Stamenkovic
Cover Image: https://pixabay.com/en/beard-business-walking-businessman-2365810/

Edited by:

CZYK Publishing Since 2011.

50 Things to Know
Visit our website at www.50thingstoknow..com

Lock Haven, PA
All rights reserved.
ISBN: 9781790916665

50 THINGS TO KNOW BOOK SERIES REVIEWS FROM READERS

I recently downloaded a couple of books from this series to read over the weekend thinking I would read just one or two. However, I so loved the books that I read all the six books I had downloaded in one go and ended up downloading a few more today. Written by different authors, the books offer practical advice on how you can perform or achieve certain goals in life, which in this case is how to have a better life.

The information is simple to digest and learn from, and is incredibly useful. There are also resources listed at the end of the book that you can use to get more information.

50 Things To Know To Have A Better Life: Self-Improvement Made Easy! by Dannii Cohen

---

This book is very helpful and provides simple tips on how to improve your everyday life. I found it to be useful in improving my overall attitude.

50 Things to Know For Your Mindfulness & Meditation Journey by Nina Edmondso

---

Quick read with 50 short and easy tips for what to think about before starting to homeschool.

50 Things to Know About Getting Started with Homeschool by Amanda Walton

I really enjoyed the voice of the narrator, she speaks in a soothing tone. The book is a really great reminder of things we might have known we could do during stressful times, but forgot over the years.

- HarmonyHawaii

50 Things to Know to Manage Your Stress: Relieve The Pressure and Return The Joy To Your Life

by Diane Whitbeck

There is so much waste in our society today. Everyone should be forced to read this book. I know I am passing it on to my family.

50 Things to Know to Downsize Your Life: How To Downsize, Organize, And Get Back to Basics

by Lisa Rusczyk Ed. D.

Great book to get you motivated and understand why you may be losing motivation. Great for that person who wants to start getting healthy, or just for you when you need motivation while having an established workout routine.

50 Things To Know To Stick With A Workout: Motivational Tips To Start The New You Today

by Sarah Hughes

50 THINGS TO KNOW WHEN BECOMING SUCCESSFUL

BOOK DESCRIPTION

Do you know separates successful people from everyone else?

Do you know how reach your potential when everyone else has expectations for you?

Do you know why do we hold ourselves back from reaching our true potential?

If you answered yes to any of these questions, then this book is for you as it will delve deeper in how to not only stand out from the crowd but how to remind yourself that your accomplishments are your own and no one else's. This book strives to show how what we have grown up thinking is the way to becoming successful isn't entirely the truth – if anything it's just the surface level, the baseline for finding your passion and reaching your potential

50 Things To know When Becoming Successful by Merylee Sevilla offers an approach to uncovering and demystifying the life lessons, and expectations we have grown up with believing will set us on our path to greatness, to success. While most books

would claim that everyone has the potential for success, the truth of the matter is that success is not for the faint of heart. Authentic and genuine success, the one where you are standing at the top of the pyramid is one that comes from hard work, dedication and persistence. It also takes thinking outside the box and knowing that your happiness and your accomplishments are meant for you and no one else.

In these pages you'll discover how owning your dreams, your passion and your successes will truly separate you from the crowd. How on the mission to becoming the best, one needs to realize that while there is the potential for everyone else to be successful, what will separate those from who want more in life to those who just want the status can be as simple as being true to oneself and working for their happiness and not the critics. This book will share the secret of the journey to becoming successful but more importantly this book will inspire you to forget the rules you were taught and learn to embrace and appreciate your successes – because the road may be the same for a lot of us – but the finish line will always be different and will still be unique.

By the time you finish this book, you will know to uncover your hidden potential and find that you have been successful all this time – it just took remembering that your accomplishments, no matter how big or small, were and are what makes one successful. So grab YOUR copy today and unleash the success within. You'll be glad you did.

TABLE OF CONTENTS

50 Things to Know

Book Series

Reviews from Readers

Insights To Reaching And Being Your Best

BOOK DESCRIPTION

TABLE OF CONTENTS

DEDICATION

ABOUT THE AUTHOR

INTRODUCTION

1. Success Doesn't Come Without Failures
2. Be Successful Out Of Desire Not Necessity
3. Success Is Subjective
4. Just Because You Have Money Doesn't Mean You Are Successful
5. Trying Is Better Than Giving Up
6. There Is No Success Without A Little Risk
7. Know What You Want To Achieve
8. Money Is Not The Reward, Freedom Is
9. It's Not What You Are, It's Who You Are
10. Don't Let Your Fears Hold You Back
11. Success Comes From Chances – Leaps of Faith
12. Taking Lemons And Making Lemonade
13. Your Successes' Will Speak For Themselves So You Don't Have To

14. Critics Will Always Criticize
15. True Accomplishment and Success Comes From Genuine Hard Work
16. You Have To Stick Out From The Pack
17. Extraordinary Is Better Than Ordinary
18. What Is Meant TO Be Will Be
19. There Will Always Be Haters
20. Success Comes With A Price
21. Being Successful Means Breaking A Sweat
22. It's Okay To Go Against The Grain
23. 10% Is Better Than 0%
24. Life Is Like A Box Of Chocolate - And So Is Success
25. Our Foundation For Success Comes From Networking
26. Greatness Comes From Teamwork
27. Strive To Be Motivated By Something Meaningful Other Than Money
28. Rise Above The Voices That Say 'You Can't'
29. Use Fear To Motivate Not Hinder
30. Dream Realistically And Succeeded Smartly
31. Learn From The Past To Move Forward
32. No One Owes You Anything
33. Remember The Journey And Not Just The End Goal

34. Success Can Be A Dream You Never Knew About
35. Turn Negativity Into Positivity – And Win!
36. Find What You Love And Do It
37. If You Dream It You Can Be It
38. Take Action And Make Your Own Opportunities
39. Don't Settle On Mediocrity – Go The Extra Mile
40. Fail Once, Try Again And Learn A Lesson
41. Don't Be Deceived By Success – It Can Mask Failure
42. Take The First Step Towards Success
43. Little Can Be More
44. Success Comes From Those Who Take Time To Listen
45. Be Open To Ideas, Diversity And Adversity
46. Trust Your Gut And Your Instinct
47. Be Successful With Humility
48. Compete With Yourself And Grow
49. Succeed To Lead And Be Remembered
50. Never Stop Learning And Never Stop Trying

Other Helpful Resources

50 Things to Know

DEDICATION

True wealth, success and happiness can only be achieved by balancing our business life with the duty we have to our self and to our family

– Joseph C. Junz Jr.

I dedicate this book to my beautiful wife, Emily – if it were not for her support, I would not have achieved the level of success I have now. She is my support, my foundation and she continue to inspire me. Through thick and thin, good and bad, I aspire to be more and do more because of her.

I also dedicate this book to everyone who has gone through life thinking they are unworthy of achieving more in life – who was told they would never amount to much because of their mistakes and the hand life has given them. This book is for anyone who let their fears and insecurities hold them back from reaching their true potential – I write with them in mind, and I write to tell them, success is dedication and persistence.

It isn't over till the fat lady sings – so keep on, keep on!

ABOUT THE AUTHOR

I use to think that I would never amount to much because life was meant to be easy, and anything worth having was just going to happen for me. This belief, illusion was one I woke up from and have since been on a journey of not only bettering myself but being an advocate for those who think they too won't amount to much. Life throws curve balls, puts up walls and obstacles, how we handle these roadblocks will determine our dedication and persistence to wanting to become a success.

Success is often regarded as making enough money and being a CEO; however, success is much more than that, and this is why I write about 50 Things To Know When Becoming A Success. It is not the material and tangible – it is the emotional and spiritual reward of knowing we can do so much more than we think we are capable of and what others think we can do. Break the mould, the stereotypes and expectations that others put and do what makes you happy. Simple enough and yet – it is a hard lesson to apply in our own lives.

Work not for the money and fame, work for personal growth, development and more importantly – work to succeed and be happy in your life.

Presently, I write and do public speaking engagements on Mental Health, LGBTQ issues and inclusion as well as chair a national committee.

For my many ramblings and insights on life, love, politics and more – I can be found on Twitter at @drMlee

INTRODUCTION

*I always wanted to be somebody,
but now I realize I should have
been more specific.*

– Lily Tomlin

Ask anyone what success is, and you will find that there are two sides to it – there is the idea that success comes from hard work and then you will hear the argument that success is just luck. I would argue it is a combination of the two and more. Success comes from hard work, dedication and persistence but it also has a factor of luck in that sometimes, you need the stars to align and for everything to be just perfect for that break.

Along with trying to determine what success, this question will also show a side of what people perceive to be a success. To some, success is working and making money to others success is making a career out of their passion and to others – success is knowing neither work nor money but a feeling of accomplishment. The sense of knowing they overcame a fear, an obstacle, to them that is a success and something that cannot be bought.

It is, for this reason, the message of this book is to spread the notion that success is in the eye of the beholder. There is no straightforward definition of what success is from one person to another because what is seen as success to one can be perceived as a failure to the other. In a way, this book looks to demystify those life lessons, these preconceived notions that success isn't meant for everyone – because it is. Success, no matter how big or small can be achieved so long as they are determined, passionate and remember never to give up when things get tough. Failure happens, it is how we move forward, how we pick ourselves up that separates the successful from the unsuccessful.

Know your dream, know what is a success for you, and you will attain it. Break a sweat, fail and learn, you will find a new level of growth and development in yourself that you never thought possible but more importantly, remember that success is so much more than the number in our bank account, or the cars and brands we have. Success is what we make it and what we want for it to be.

1. SUCCESS DOESN'T COME WITHOUT FAILURES

Failure is success in progress

– Albert Einstein

So often it is assumed that our successes can only happen when we don't fail – wrong. The truth is, any achievements that I have encountered in my own life have come after a failure, a disappointment and while though it can be hard to accept and embrace, when we take a moment to look back, it is all that has gone wrong time and time again that has propelled us to be where we are. I often will think and wonder if I had chosen a different path, or made a different decision, would I be where I am today and I know the truth is, no, I would not be where I am today nor would I have found the success I have today. At times, we will think our failures are signs to give up, the truth is, we must take these failures and learn from them. There is a reason they say "trial and error" and it is because success doesn't come without failure.

2. BE SUCCESSFUL OUT OF DESIRE NOT NECESSITY

Find somebody to be successful for. Raise their hopes. Think of their needs

– Barack Obama

For much of my life I strived for success that was merely my own – the truth of the matter is, my success came when I had someone I wanted to be successful for. It is important though not to confuse or think of this as a means to strive for approval – if anything it should be seen as a way of wanting to be the best person that this person or persons know in you. In my life, I thought success meant doing it for others in an attempt to gain their recognition and approval; however, it wasn't until I found my partner who nurtured my dreams and aspirations that I realized what I was striving for was not only unhealthy, but it was the wrong way to go about becoming successful. The drive I thought I had was more of an obligation, a necessity – but, when I found someone who saw the potential in me, saw what I had to offer, then my success became about self-discovery and trust. It was a trust that I was capable of meeting their hopes and aspirations while still being true to myself.

When we are younger, we take our successes and use it to gain recognition, to gain the attention of our parents, our peers, friends and colleagues. As we get older, this habit of being successful for recognition becomes something that suddenly consumes us, and when we fail or have short-comings, we are ashamed of ourselves and fearful of what those around us will think of us. True success though comes from a desire, from passion and not out of necessity or obligation. Success is not achieved for the sole purpose of being respected because every act, every job, everything one did get where they are will be recognized without being flaunted. Those who matter will acknowledge and be proud of your success and accomplishments, those who don't matter in your life – will critique, downplay and possibly bring you down. Success, no matter how big or small is always celebrated.

3. SUCCESS IS SUBJECTIVE

*My secret for success? I don't
know what the hell success means*

– Al Lewis

I use to think that there was a "clear" definition of what success was – then again, if we look at celebrities and those who are successful and of whom we aspire to we think we can do as they did. We use their accomplishments and what they've done to get where they are as a means of measuring our own success – I was wrong. I was wrong to think that I could take the formula of success of another and use it to not only create my own success but as a form of measuring it as well.

We often think that success is not only easy to measure but that it can be easily replicated – the truth of the matter is that success is subjective. There is no cookie-cutter approach, and for the most part, another man's success could actually be another is the idea of failure. Success should never be measured against anyone else is expectations, it should be measured to one's own expectations. This is a lesson that was a hard one to accept and learn from. For much of my adult life, I thought that success was all the same, and it was not till I began to see and embrace my accomplishments that I realized success is indeed in the eye of the beholder.

4. JUST BECAUSE YOU HAVE MONEY DOESN'T MEAN YOU ARE SUCCESSFUL

Success is not what you have,
but who you are

– Bo Bennett

We live in a day and age where everything is material based. Our wealth is measured in monetary value, and our successes to are measured in what we have as well. True success though is not how much you have but really if you as a person have grown and developed. I have always correlated success with a promotion, a raise – a reward. I never saw success as a pat on the back, as someone else learning from my skills and applying it to their own life – no, to me, success was measured in the tangible, the visual.

Taking a moment and looking at the top elites of the world – some come from old money, some come from hard work, and some come from mere luck and smart investing. Three ways to wealth and riches, are they all successful? Some would argue yes, while others would say no. Why? Because luck is not a success, it is lucky. It is important to realize that just because that just because that penny stock has turned your hundreds to thousands if not millions that you are successful. Success comes from hard work, aspiration and dedication. Others would also argue that those who come from old money aren't successful – I would say that they have more to prove that the hard work because of the expectations, the standards they are now held to.

Never see success has how much is in your bank account, in your wallet, or the car and house you have – see success as, who will remember you for your drive, your passion and hard work. That is the real success.

5. TRYING IS BETTER THAN GIVING UP

Success consists of going from failure to failure without loss of enthusiasm

– Winston Churchill

In high school I had barely passed Grade 12 math – to this day I wonder how I even did pass it given much of my exams were below 50% and yet, I passed. Exam after exam I struggled to excel like my peers but when I finished the course and passed – THAT was a success. While at times I found myself frustrated and ready to wave the white flag, I still persevered, I still was determined to try and continue because I believed I would pass, that I would succeed, and I did.

In life we think that when we fail, we should give up because there is no way we will be successful – those who give up without a fight those are the ones who will never know or aspire to become successful. It is those who despite hitting roadblock after roadblock, obstacle after obstacle that push through that succeed – those are the successful ones. They are the ones who still pick themselves up and continue – sure, they will have their bad days, their moments of anger and frustration, but there is also within them a fire, a drive. It is both of these that brew success – it is what differentiates a successful person versus a failure.

Some of the greatest minds and inventors that our world has ever seen and come to know succeeded because of their persistence to their failures. The Wright Brothers had they given up their numerous attempts to fly we may have never seen the airplane take off. What we have and use today, the telephone, the TV and even the lightbulb – the technology which has simplified our lives, these came from continual testing and continual trials. Imagine had these men given up, imagine if they had decided to call it quits after their first attempt. Success is taking your failures and never giving up.

6. THERE IS NO SUCCESS WITHOUT A LITTLE RISK

*Only those who dare to fail
greatly can ever achieve greatly*

– Robert F. Kennedy

Growing up I remember being in elementary and seeing a motivational poster that said, Dare to Dream. I never understood this saying until I entered high school and it was then that I realized what it meant. Dare to dream is about taking a risk, pushing the limits and the boundaries to achieve something more significant. Success has never come from playing it safe, it has never come from taking the easy paved path – success comes from taking a risk and becoming vulnerable

Success is about not only owning your mistakes and failures, but it is about staying steadfast to them as well – because so often when we feel that we are going against the grain, it is almost easier to go with the flow than to be our own person. The movements taking place today around the world, whether it be the movement to end homophobia, to combat racism or to share a voice in the MeToo movement – these came from people who dared to fall in an attempt to achieve something more significant.

7. KNOW WHAT YOU WANT TO ACHIEVE

*Before anything else,
preparation is the key to success*

– Alexander Graham Bell

Life is unpredictable – there are many ups and downs, turns and sometimes roadblocks, but despite all these, it is essential that when we are working towards a goal, we know precisely what that end state is. I am a planner – more specifically, I like to have what I call a game plan. Sometimes these game plans go off without a hitch, and sometimes these game plans result in multiple revisions but the end state for which I use these game plans for remain consistent.

I think most people would argue that success comes without preparation and I say that is bollocks. Success comes from hard work, planning and development. And, if one takes a moment to think and reflect on their own accomplishments, their own accomplishments, they will realize that it was not random (and if it was, bravo, I hope you'll share that secret!) but rather, it came from knowing what they wanted and how to were going to get there.

Imagine working in the corporate world, depending on the industry it can be a dog-eat-dog world; however, carefully planning how you plan to stick out from the pack and how you plan to demonstrate your skills and asset makes you a planner. Successful people plan their days, whether it is what they will do on the weekend or how to manage multiple meetings on a Monday. I have learned that for my own successes, planning is what separates those from who deserve success to those who merely want it for the reward, the glory and nothing else.

8. MONEY IS NOT THE REWARD, FREEDOM IS

*Money won't create success, the
freedom to make it will*

– `Nelson Mandela

Growing up, I use to think that money and wealth was a sign of success; however, as I have grown, matured and learned to discover my passion, money is not the reward if anything it can be an obstacle, a distraction. So often we are consumed by this notion that money can buy happiness and it's not unrealistic because society pushes this belief as well. The truth of the matter is money can be more of a curse than a blessing. It can cause more aches and grief than be a positive and rewarding thing.

So often I find that we can be blinded if not consumed with wanting to attain a sign of wealth that is greater than others but the truth of the matter is, that is not success. Real success comes when you have the freedom from being obligated to do something. The best example is to look at investors, self-made millionaires or those who have managed to work to the point that they have the luxury of going on extended holidays – the real value of success is not money but time. Time to do as one pleases and feel as though there is no guilt. When we allow ourselves not to be controlled by money or the frivolous things, only then can we say that we have found success.

9. IT'S NOT WHAT YOU ARE, IT'S WHO YOU ARE

How many cares one loses when one decides not to be something but to be someone

– Coco Chanel

Growing up I was raised to have pride in my name, but I was also taught also to take pride in my accomplishments and the fact that my parents worked hard to establish our family name. As I got older and began to navigate my way through life and build my own reputation and successes, I learned that it's not what I am but rather who I am. It can be hard to distinguish between who and what when it comes to success because they seem one of the same. The truth is, what you are is often associated with a name, a reputation, it is sometimes bestowed upon us, who we are is what one has accomplished to be recognized and remembered.

I grew up not seeing the difference and thinking what and who I was were the same thing – but I've come to learn that what matters most is not what we are, but who. Who we are, how we are remembered, the kind and selfless acts we do, those are the things that are recognized and what dictate our successes. Who we are speaks louder than what.

10. DON'T LET YOUR FEARS HOLD YOU BACK

Those who are successful overcome their fears and take action. Those who don't submit to their concerns and live with regrets

– Jay-Z

There is an old mantra that encourages people always to do one thing that scares them. I believe this, and I think this is what separates those who are successful from those who are not – the risks, the leap of faith, the taking a chance even when we are scared. I will never admit my fears openly or to anyone, and yet, I know that my worries are what has propelled me to become who I am. Much of my accomplishments have come from my fears, from risks and leaps.

One of my biggest fears that have resulted in my most significant successes and accomplishments was when I fully embraced myself and fully allowed myself to be me. For some, they knew they were gay at a very young age; however, I had to go through the motions of being a teenager and a young adult to embrace myself fully but more importantly realize that my sexuality did not dictate my future let alone my accomplishments.

The moment I embraced my sexuality, the moment I decided not to care or allow what others think of me get in the way of my future – I found myself not only thriving but seeing my own successes. The moment we allow our fears to hold us back, to control us, it is the moment we limit ourselves. When we let fear win or control us, we allow it to take over and dictate how we go about in life. I found that the moment I allowed myself to see past my fears, to move forward and in doing so I have found not only happiness but success.

11. SUCCESS COMES FROM CHANCES – LEAPS OF FAITH

*We must walk consciously only
part way toward our goal, and then
leap in the dark to our success*

– Henry David Thoreau

While I may not be one to jump on chances as they come, if there is one lesson that I have learned on my way to finding and becoming successful is that success comes from a leap of faith. It happens when we take the route of that we have planned for ourselves and take on the opportunities that present themselves. This is not to say that one should take shortcuts or the easy route, what this means is sometimes along our way to greatness we will find ourselves with an opportunity – a chance.

In my experience I have always been skeptical to anything that veered me off my path to success; however, through trial and error, I have come to learn that sometimes, when we go on our way to our end goal, we are thrown a line. This line is sometimes that needed push that helps we need when we are feeling despair or want to give up. The goals we set to lead us to our successes – sometimes that leap of faith, that jump into the unknown is what is needed. In life, I have found that when I have closed my eyes and just taken that leap, amazing things begin to unfold, opportunities that once didn't exist now present themselves. Success is like that – we work through life paying our dues when a chance appears. A break – I have learned to embrace this and let life happen, and let success because sometimes, success is not only worked towards but unexplained.

12. TAKING LEMONS AND MAKING LEMONADE

Success is relative. It is what we can make of the mess we have made of things

– T.S. Eliot

No one likes when obstacles appear in their seemingly easy journey let alone when things don't go as they planned. We work towards our successes, and sometimes I find that we become blinded by this illusion and believe the journey is to be smooth and effortless and without friction, the truth is – anything worth having takes time, takes patience, and it takes hard work. Not only does it require patience, hard work and time but it also takes innovation to be able to make whatever may come and go with the punches.

It is so easy to see when things go wrong and to automatically give up; however, real success and what differentiates one from the pack is when they can take a problem and see if not create a solution. In a way I can attribute my successes to this – to this approach and mentality of perseverance, in seeing past the problem and looking towards a solution. When you reach a level of success – you realize that no matter the obstacle, no matter the issue, one can always handle the matter at hand. Whatever the problem, whatever the barrier, it is about seeing the bright side when things seem dark and impossible.

13. YOUR SUCCESSES' WILL SPEAK FOR THEMSELVES SO YOU DON'T HAVE TO

Be careful, ever so careful, in trumpeting your own achievements, and always talk less about yourself than about other people. Modesty is generally preferable

– Robert Greene

I remember in grade school how whenever my teacher would return our exam results everyone would compare and then either boast about how easy the test was or make excuses as to why they did not do as well. Growing up I bared this mentality of comparing my successes, and the hard work that went to achieving these outcomes – little did I know or realize was that no matter what the task was, someone who is successful never brags, boasts or justifies their successes (or shortcomings to it). This was a lesson that I did not learn until I began my first internship working in government within the communications and social media section. I was in my early 20's and had always been innovative and was often considered that person that thought outside the box.

During my time working in this section, I challenged myself by continually learning about new approaches and methods of expanding and having a more extensive reach when it came to social media. I was self-motivated and driven – then again, I was heavily involved in social media from a personal perspective. I had a Facebook, Twitter, MySpace – any form of social media I had an account for and it was because of this involvement that I began to demonstrate my skills and knowledge and how this could benefit my work in the office. For weeks and months, the only acknowledgement of my work and effort was a simple "Approve" and a signature – but still, I saw this as a success, as a sign I was on the right path. While the numbers and the data showed my approach to communications was thriving better than their previous plan, while I wanted to say "Look, it's working!" I bit my tongue and decided to continue on with my work. It is so easy to want to boast, to want to say "I told you so!" when we know something to be true and right; however, what speaks louder than these statements are the results. It was not until my last day working in the office that they had talked about my accomplishments and the work I had done, all of a sudden what I had looked for in those years I had worked there I was now getting in one afternoon. It was a humbling moment to know that my persistence and my instinct to go about a certain way was being recognized but also, while I wanted to boast and get credit, they were giving me credit through various projects and responsibilities.

Sometimes, we will want to speak out and get what we think is our deserved recognition and appreciation but someone who is genuinely successful won't care whether their hard work is acknowledged or appreciated – because deep down they know it's true. While we may feel like we are going unnoticed in our day-to-day work, remember that good work never goes unnoticed and unrecognized, no matter what.

14. CRITICS WILL ALWAYS CRITICIZE

If I tell you I'm good, probably you will say I'm boasting. But if I tell you I'm not good, you'll know I'm lying

– Bruce Lee

No matter what we do, we will always find ourselves being criticized and judged. From the clothes we wear to the car we drive and even how we make decisions, there is still someone who will step up and critique. Sometimes the comments will be positive, sometimes negative and sometimes they will just be statements – but critics will always criticize. When we become successful, we sometimes believe and think that others will be happy for us, that they would only want for us to be successful, but this is not always true. When we show our accomplishments, whether we want to or not, someone will still jump at the opportunity to question if not counter the achievements and yet on the other hand, if we are nonchalant and are humble about our success and accomplishments, we are said to be silently boasting.

It is essential to keep in mind that no matter what we do, sometimes knowing we are successful, knowing that we have accomplished something is better than anyone else trying to take it away. For example, if we get a job promotion over our colleague, they may feel bitter and say the only reason for your promotion is because you are friends with your boss rather than congratulate and see you received it based on merit. Another way that others critic is when we chose to not create a scene (even a positive one) and all of a sudden, not saying we got a promotion is seen as being manipulative and sneaky – when again, this isn't the case.

Success can be fickle for some, and sometimes it can bring out the worst rather than the best which in a way is what distinguishes a successful person from not. Someone who is successful or is on the path to becoming successful will know that while it would be nice always to have the support of our colleagues and friends, this isn't still the case and we should never take it too personally. Our successes are our own and no one else.

15. TRUE ACCOMPLISHMENT AND SUCCESS COMES FROM GENUINE HARD WORK

Success is only meaningful and enjoyable if it feels like your own

– Michelle Obama

My first real job came when I entered university – what made it my first real job was that it was one that I got on my own and without the help or influence of others. It was a great accomplishment and, in a way, it was a great morale booster as I had achieved it on my own. Success sometimes seems to be perceived as something that should be at the ownership everyone else but our own; however, the truth of the matter is that success comes from genuine hard work but also success is for no one else is pleasure but one's own.

So often we work towards a goal and hope that this accomplishment and these successes we work towards will make those around us happy and proud of us. This is not the case if anything it is an illusion we are told because success achieved for others is an excellent motivator as opposed to the progress made for ourselves. I think that the moment we realize and accept our successes as our own, only then can we truly enjoy it. Success is hard work, it is dedication, but more importantly, it is our own and no one else's.

16. YOU HAVE TO STICK OUT FROM THE PACK

The Ladder of success is never crowded at the top

– Napoleon Hill

My favorite game to play is chess – for some they see is as dull, very long and drawn out; however, to me, it is a game of strategy and wit both of which I enjoy thoroughly. When it comes to chess though, it can be easily paralleled to that of success and how reaching the top is one that requires strategy and wit. When I found my niche in life and my strongest points, I realized that while the climb to the top begins with many in a pond – it eventually narrows out at the top because the truth is, success isn't for everyone.

Some of the greatest minds and the most successful people in the world and of whom I admire – from Bill Gates to Donald Trump and Elon Musk, while these men sometimes had wild ideas, they stuck out from the pack by always being a step and a plan ahead. Once they had their million-dollar idea and they stuck to it, they stuck out from the pack and eventually found themselves in a league of their own. My successes and accomplishments have placed me in a league of my own because success is one that is personal, that is unique and one that can't be copied. Everyone looks for that quick-buck idea; however, not everyone has that persistence and drive which is why it will never be crowded at the top.

17. EXTRAORDINARY IS BETTER THAN ORDINARY

If you are not willing to risk the usual, you will have to settle for the ordinary

– Jim Rohn

Growing up, I remember how anyone who did not fit the mold which our community and well, the society set out they were considered "weird." From the way they dressed to their physical appearance, they were considered the misfits. As I got older, I began to realize that these so-called misfits were the ones who stuck out not in a wrong way but actually in a positive manner. It seems that the ones who were considered weird were the ones who grew up being successful because they thought outside the box. They were the ones who saw beyond the limitations, the stereotypes and made it their own.

I was never considered a misfit if anything I was able to fit in with both the popular and these very group of people who would be game-changers later in life from the skater-boy who became a well-known DJ to the average math-nerd who created a million-dollar business. These so-called misfits took their image, and how everyone saw them as and used it to their advantage, they used it to become the success that they are now. In my case, I used my ability to empathize and speak up for wrongs to be right and became a success. I used it, and that has become my success. While I never belonged to a group, it took me realizing that sticking out was not only okay but sometimes being extraordinary is where the best ideas come from.

18. WHAT IS MEANT TO BE WILL BE

Success is a science, if you have the conditions, you get the result.

– Oscar Wilde

I used to believe that if I followed to a T what my idols were doing, I too could be successful – heck, you've purchased this book with the hopes that you also will uncover your real potential and become a success. Here is a little secret that I learned after failing – success can't be replicated, and no matter how many times I try to do precisely as Richard Branson or Elon Musk, I will never be like them let alone amass that same level of success. It isn't because I don't have ideas or that I'm not creative, I am – the difference is though sometimes, success has to be (as much as I hate to say it) left up to fate.

Why fate? Why can't we follow the same steps and become successful?

Simple – because it takes certain conditions and timing before everything works out. I may not be one who believes in stars aligning; however, I have learned in my 30 years of living that sometimes there is no other plausible answer than the "perfect timing" paired with dedication and perseverance.

What is meant to will be when the timing is right. As Oscar Wilde says it, success is a science, and it indeed is true.

19. THERE WILL ALWAYS BE HATERS

The worst part of success is to try finding someone who is happy for you

– Bette Midler

When it comes to boys and girls, girls are straight up mean. When you pair this meanness to success – it is even worse. In school and early on in my career, I would feel bad for any of my accomplishments that were my own and not my teams. I would feel bad and try to make them feel as though the recognition I received personally also included them; however, the reality was, they either did not do anything or they genuinely did not deserve it.

The truth of the matter is when you are successful or on the way to becoming the best that you can be, not only will there be critics but there will always be someone who won't be happy for your accomplishments and successes. What one needs to remember is that along the journey to the top – those who matter will not only show their support but will genuinely be happy for you no matter what. Haters will always hate and while I use to be a people pleaser, I have learned that life is too short to be pleasing those who actually don't mean anything or have any significance in our life – let alone who are toxic to our well-being.

When we reach a level of success that is our peak, it is important to surround ourselves with positivity and with support, anything else would truly be sabotaging our true potential.

20. SUCCESS COMES WITH A PRICE

The only question to ask yourself is, how much are you willing to sacrifice to achieve this success?

– Larry Flynt

Sidney Crosby, Steve Jobs and Lady Gaga– what do they all have in common? They have all reached their level of success through hard work and making sacrifices in their personal lives.

At 27 years of age, I found myself at a crossroad- live a life with the minimal expectation of myself and from others and striving for more and becoming something. At this point I had written a book, I had managed to be remembered for my accomplishments and actions; however, I wasn't sure if there was more I wanted.

During the summer of 2014, I embarked on a journey of enlightenment in Spain. I decided that I would walk over 600 km across the country because for one, no one thought I could and secondly, I had the time to. During this walk or rather journey, I had this epiphany reflecting on aspects of my life – from relationships to personal and professional aspirations. It was when I began to break down what I had succeeded in and those who were there (or not there) for me that at one point I had made a sacrifice. I moved across a country to go to school – it was a move that I thought would be temporary; however, after graduating, I decided to relocate to my new city and pave my own way. This was a decision that not only helped my career, but it was a decision that meant sacrificing relationships with friends and family in my hometown.

In a way, this is why they say we should surround ourselves with like-minded people, with those who are confident and supportive because when we make a sacrifice, those who are still there by our side through it all, those are the ones who are meant to be there. Life is full of decisions, and the truth is each decision sometimes has a component of sacrifice attached if not hidden within it. Our future, our destiny means making those hard decisions and recognizing the sacrifices we make knowing that we are working towards our dream, our future and our happiness and success.

21. BEING SUCCESSFUL MEANS BREAKING A SWEAT

I'm not one of those people who thinks they simply deserve success. I have the drive to work

– Bridget Moynahan

Up until high school, I played sports – I was lucky in a way because the games I excelled in did not require much effort from me. I was fortunate enough that I had a natural aptitude in sports I chose; however, when I entered University and attempted these same sports that I excelled in, I realized I was no longer excelling. This realization applied to many other facets in my life and in a way, it was a lesson I did not want to believe – the lesson being: success means putting in the effort and not just costing.

If we look at professional athletes and their lifestyle, those who are the top tier of their sport are the ones who eat and sleep their sport. They spend hours a day perfecting their art and working to distinguish themselves. This is easily and truthfully very much applicable to life and one's journey to becoming a success. Students, professionals, no matter one's title – those who want to separate themselves from the pack will work day and night to show how much better they are. It is this dedication that separates the successful from the unsuccessful. As they say, hard work requires a little blood and sweat.

22. IT'S OKAY TO GO AGAINST THE GRAIN

A man who wants to lead the orchestra must turn his back on the crowd

– Unknown

Growing up I was never one to do things by the book – in a way, this was seen as me going against the grain, swimming against the flow of things to not only find myself but for the most part, I enjoyed going to the beat of my own drum. This action though, for the most part, is often seen as being a rule-breaker, a rebel. We learn there is a reason that things are done a certain way, the rules and procedures of things happen because someone, somewhere has gone through the motions to create a flow of stability. Rules are meant to be followed not broken or bent; however, this does not apply to success and the journey. No journey is the same, nor is the journey one that follows a linear structure.

Conforming to rules and societal expectations can sometimes result in a cookie-cutter approach and lifestyle. The thing with conformity is it means we follow the flow of things and we all think and do the same things – even vying for success. This poses a problem because as we know, the top of the chain for those who are successful and those who are not is not a crowded place if anything it is only a small and select group of people. The reason? Because they went against the grain, whether that was sticking out from the crowd or walking to the beat of their own drum – they did not let societal expectations and conformity rule and dictated their path and future.

23. 10% IS BETTER THAN 0%

Those who try to do something and fail are infinitely better than those who try nothing and succeed.

– Lloyd Jones

At a very young age, I suffered from depression which meant that sometimes what is easy and straightforward for others is a struggle and sometimes an uphill battle for myself. In a way battling depression, along with my other short-comings, I worked extra hard and put in more effort than most would when it came to everyday tasks. The older I became and had the support I had around me, I learned that despite my struggles, despite everything that seemed to stack against me – my efforts made me stand out from those who always put in their 110%.

It is this realization that not only is effort subjective but just as success is personal so is the effort. Though some would and could judge me and say that I could try a little harder or put in more effort – the fact that I tried was better than not. In a way, this was a life lesson that I would learn and always remind myself. Success is subjective, it is personal, no one can say this is the level success you are to work towards or what you are limited to; therefore, if progress is personal then why not the effort, the trying we do?

Putting in 50% is better than 0% - waking up and saying "I got this" is better than saying "I give up." Appreciating and acknowledging one's successes and accomplishments is better than ignoring and undermining one's strengths. When it comes to the journey to becoming successful, we have to remember what we should be for ourselves and not anyone else is.

24. LIFE IS LIKE A BOX OF CHOCOLATE - AND SO IS SUCCESS

If you try a bunch of things, you often learn more from failure than success.

– Elon Musk

One of my favorite movies to watch is Forrest Gump – one because the main character, which is played by Tom Hanks is a simple townie who accomplishes so much and yet never understands the magnitude of his success. From saving a fellow soldier to the marathon and eventually being a father – his simple-minded approach to things demonstrate how success is indeed in the eye of the beholder. Just as life like a box of chocolate, so is the success. Sometimes we work through things and think they are just everyday accomplishments – ordinary; however, what we need to see and realize is that success can be varied. They can be significant, small, they can be as simple as finishing a task and winning a certificate – the truth is our accomplishments can sometimes be what we least expect and think.

When we take our time and enjoy the journey to becoming the best version of ourselves and enjoy our achievements, we have to also bring with it our failures. The obstacles, the thorns we wish never sidetracked us on our mission and goal actually play a more significant role in our journey than we expected. The truth of the matter is when it comes to our failures, they are the most significant lessons from which we learn from. I have learned more from my mistakes and failures than I have from my accomplishments. I have learned more from what not to do than to do.

Once we have reached a level of success in our own personal lives, we learn that success was only possible the moment we celebrated both failures and successes no matter how big or small they are.

25. OUR FOUNDATION FOR SUCCESS COMES FROM NETWORKING

Our success has really been based on partnerships from the very beginning

– Bill Gates

While the journey to the top may sometimes be a struggle and lonely – the way to honestly know our strengths and maximizing our achievements means knowing when to network and when to be okay with reaching out for guidance and insight. I use to think that when it comes to networking that this was a sign I needed help, that I could not achieve success without it. In reality, those who are successful do need help, and they know that the only way to get to the top is to network, more specifically, network with like minds and those who they aspire to be and become.

Without networking, without some form of foundation to guide us to where we want to be, how can we genuinely accomplish success? We can't. What we can do is work towards what we want, know what it is we want to accomplish and strive for but sometimes what we need though is that helping hand – that guidance and support to help us achieve this. Networking may be stressful for some who prefer to work alone or think that success is meant to be done solo – this isn't the case. Like the old adage, it takes a village to raise a child – it takes a team and support to be successful.

26. GREATNESS COMES FROM TEAMWORK

Success comes when people act together; failure tends to happen alone

– Deepak Chopra

When a collective group of people who have the same goals and aspirations come together, they become unstoppable, but they also accomplish what they set out to do because they have worked with those with the same vision. Some might confuse this with striving for success that is others; however, the main difference is, the success is one that everyone shares in. For example, Skip the Dishes is a Canadian application that was created by two brothers and their friend. The brothers saw a problem or rather a lack of use of maximizing technology to simplify the process of take-out. While the brothers both had the ideas and the concept, they had to turn to their friends who were knowledgeable in application creation and coding to actually get it to come off the ground.

While we should remember that our successes should be our own, sometimes we will meet others who also share in our vision which not only can be rewarding, but it can be the support we wish and want for. When we isolate ourselves, when we choose to not share or talk with others we not only isolate ourselves but we hinder any natural flow of ideas and greatness.

Success may be our own, but it is always sweeter when we can share it with like minds and like visionaries.

27. STRIVE TO BE MOTIVATED BY SOMETHING MEANINGFUL OTHER THAN MONEY

Don't think money does everything or you are going to end up doing everything for money

– Voltaire

Money doesn't buy happiness – it can buy things that make us happy, but that does not always equate happiness. I had found that now that I am married have a home and responsibilities that my priorities are not as they once were 5 or 6 years ago when I was single. When it comes to my personal and professional life, and what I want to accomplish I try to look beyond the money. This is easier said than done because if we all had a little more in our accounts our lives might be a little easier; however when you focus on achievements, goals and dreams where the reward is something other than the money you begin to discover a new level of enlightenment and happiness.

When we are looking to become successful, the first thing that comes to mind is money, wealth the material things that can showcase we have made it. I grew up very fortunate, my parents provided for my brothers and I. They worked to ensure we got whatever we wanted and needed in life. As I got older and began to see the world through life-experiences, I realized money is not the only reward. Other things that are just as valuable as money are happiness – happiness in knowing that I was pursuing a passion and being as true to myself as I could be.

I think of artists, whether they are musicians or painters who sometimes jeopardize their values to gain notoriety and fame. Sometimes they do this to get that break, and then once they've amassed a level of success they'll pursue their real passion and happiness; however, sometimes, this isn't always the case, and their accomplishments are for no one other than those who veered them from their goal.

Yes, we need money to buy things – but we should remember that money can also ruin our passion and dedication and make success feel like a failure. This is when we need to remind ourselves to be inspired and motivated by something else other than money.

28. RISE ABOVE THE VOICES THAT SAY 'YOU CAN'T'

If you hear a voice within you say 'you cannot paint,' then by all means paint, and that voice will be silenced

– Vincent Van Gogh

On the journey to achieving greatness and success, we will find that there is always someone to critique and judge which is why when it comes to our own critique and judgement we have to learn to rise above it. When it comes to the journey, there will be times we encounter obstacles some as obvious as our friends or our competitors not wanting us to succeed to more often than not, our own judgement and critique. The voices, the negative thinking, the judgement and beliefs that say we can't, are the first and really foremost biggest reason some find themselves never accomplishing or meeting their real potential.

The solution?

We have to train ourselves, our minds and break that chain of negativity because once we are able to acknowledge if not break this cycle, only then can take the first step and silence these critics. This isn't easy, I find it difficult because if all your life you have worked to strive to please others and claim the accomplishments reached for them as your own – it is a hard habit to break. Habits are hard, not judging and selling ourselves short is even harder. When we take the time and challenge these beliefs – turn the cants to can, the results can be shocking. Not only can they be surprising but they can be uplifting and empowering because suddenly there is this newfound courage and strength to achieve a new level of greatness but also independence.

Success requires hard work – why complicate the journey through negative thinking and doubt?

29. USE FEAR TO MOTIVATE NOT HINDER

Do one thing every day that scares you

– Eleanor Roosevelt

On the journey to the top, life will be full of decisions. Some decisions will be easy choices while others will be harder. In life though, it is the hard decisions we have to make that motivate and inspire us to a new level of success. I have found that by taking chances, the outcomes have led to more significant opportunities and prospects. Why? Because uncertainty can actually be a strong motivator to try something new and venture to the unknown.

When we find ourselves in a situation where our seemingly perfectly planned journey to success throws us a curve ball – some will concede while others would take on the challenge and uncertainty with confidence because it's these obstacles that can weed out those who aren't cut out to be successful in life and in their dream. As Eleanor Roosevelt once said, do one thing every day that scares you, and this statement is not only as accurate as true but inspiring as well. When we can take what life throws us by the horn and showcase our ability not only to adapt but be resilient – we do thrive and succeed.

Doing one thing every day may be hard to do – but taking a risk once in a while and stepping out of one's comfort zone can be a strong and true success

30. DREAM REALISTICALLY AND SUCCEEDED SMARTLY

If you set your goals ridiculously high and it's a failure, you will fail above everyone else's success.

– James Cameron

When I was younger I wanted to be an astronaut because I was passionate about stars and space, but I also thought going up on a spaceship would be cool. This dream lasted up until I entered high school and realized what it took to succeed was, by my standards not my cup of tea. I began to re-evaluate my life and what it was I wanted to do. I thought about my passions, my hobbies and decided that law and politics interested me; therefore, that was the field I would work towards.

My senior year of high school we were asked to create a mock life plan of where we saw ourselves in 5 years and then 10 years. This was to factor in post-secondary education and then entering the real world, in other words, finding a profession, a career. As I created my life plan using my interest in law and politics, at 18 years of age, I thought I had life figured out. Wrong.

While visiting my family during a school break, I found this assignment and I began to reflect on what I had planned for myself – based on my writings I was to have been successful by the time I turned 24. I was not. I was still in school working on my degree which was far from my initial plan. I was not studying law or politics, I was studying psychology. I was not going to become a lawyer or politician, I did not know what I was going to do for my career. Reflecting on this I realize that sometimes our aspirations and dreams can be far-fetched, unrealistic. We take our dreams and create a game plan for how to achieve this – sometimes though, these plans are optimistic rather than realistic.

Once I had reached a level success and happiness, I realized that it was important to be realistic within the optimism and visionary approach. It is always easier to look at life through rose-colored glasses but the truth is, success is seen through compassion, understanding and truth.

31. LEARN FROM THE PAST TO MOVE FORWARD

Don't live life in the past lane

– Samantha Ettus

One of my greatest flaws and quite possibly a weakness of mine is my inability to learn from my past but also to not be able to move on from it. More often than not I will often allow myself to be held back by something that I have experienced in my past and for most, this past experience is one that is traumatic or that has defined who they are as a person. For me, I allowed my past and the disappointments that I thought I had done to those who expected so much from me to control me and the decisions I made for my future. I allowed it to not only dictate my life but I allowed it to hold me back from any true potential I had in becoming successful

– I allowed my past make me a prisoner and a burden to anyone around me.

The reality was that as I matured, as I discovered who around me were my true friends and true allies, I began to allow myself to move on from my past. I began to take my past experiences – no matter how positive or negative they were to motivate me, to inspire me but more importantly, my past became a reminder of who I did not want to become and who and where I wanted to be in life. In a way, when I became successful and reached this level of comfort and appreciation I realized that allowing my past to hold me back was harming no one but myself and because of this, I learned to move past it. I learned to learn from the past, no matter how painful, traumatic or how much I would rather close the door and use it to look forward.

32. NO ONE OWES YOU ANYTHING

*Don't go around saying the
world owes you a living. The world
owes you nothing. It was here first.*

– Mark Twain

I am part of a generation that is often regarded as being entitled and privileged. My generation (Millennials) are followed by the iGeneration, another group of individuals that also believe that life and society owe them something. What does this mean? When it comes to achieving success, these generations feel as though the world and society owe them something. What does this say? It means that two generations feel as though hard work does not need to be exerted when it comes to being successful if anything it should just be handed to them.

A success that isn't earned is never as perfect as one perceives or thinks and this is something I do believe. Anything worth having never comes easy nor does it happen without a bit of work. This mentality and mindset is one that has corrupted an entire generation to thinking and believing that whatever successes they are to get is to be given and not earned. This type of success – the one that comes not from hard work is never as sweet as one imagines.

While I have spent much of my life believing that success was given and not earned, now as an adult I have learned that progress is best made and achieved through hard work and dedication. Millionaires never stop earning after they've earned their first million nor do they feel that the world owes them anything. That is success, and that is what differentiates someone from the successful and unsuccessful.

33. REMEMBER THE JOURNEY AND NOT JUST THE END GOAL

The journey is the reward

– Chinese Proverb

A Few years back I embarked on the Camino de Santiago, it is a walking pilgrimage through Spain where at the end you are asked what the reason for your journey. There are three options: spiritual, mental and physical. I embarked on the Camino for spiritual and mental reasons – I wanted to find enlightenment and some peace. In the beginning I was walking from town to town with the focus being on reaching the end of the walk; however, I learned very quickly that the journey to Santiago would be more than just a walk – it would be life changing.

The path to success is never easy nor is it one that we often consider to be important – the reality is, the journey is the reward, the lessons that dictate how we see and do things. When it comes to being a success we think that once we achieve it, what we have to enjoy is the view from the top. The reality is, the journey to becoming a success is the reward and what dictates how successful we are and continue to be is the journey.

For me, Santiago was more than a finish line it was a life-changing journey and the success that came from my journey was one that brought me many successes. Sometimes we forget our humble beginnings and the journey – and the moment we do, we lose sight of our true successes.

34. SUCCESS CAN BE A DREAM YOU NEVER KNEW ABOUT

Follow your arrow where ever it points

– Kelly Musgrave

When I finished school, I never thought I would be working in government, let alone doing public speaking and writing articles published for others to read. These accomplishments were once what I thought impossible, only a dream, never did I think that they would be in the cards for me. At the same time, I never had any clear and definite idea of where I was supposed to go and what I was supposed to do. I had rough ideas of what I wanted in life – a good paying job and the freedom to travel, throw in a lack of responsibility. Now, my life has taken a turn where I have appreciated my achievements and harnessed my successes into a career.

Life is funny in that way – when you least expect something, or when you think it not possible suddenly everything is possible and dreams become a reality. At times we may feel the path we are on is a test of our dedication to our dreams, an examination of our persistence – oddly enough though when you know, you know. That is how fate works and how the climb to the top of the food chain plays out. Those who are meant to be successful, whether they have an idea or whether they realize it or not, will be successful. Sometimes, things play out as they are meant to be and to object or thinking otherwise can make the journey longer than it should be. This is life – this is the journey to becoming and finding our passion and success.

35. TURN NEGATIVITY INTO POSITIVITY – AND WIN!

You can't win in life if you're losing in your mind. Change your thoughts and it'll change your life

– Tony Gaskins

When we let our negative self-talk control and dominate our decisions, we allow it to hinder any possibilities of moving forward but also succeeding. Whether the negativity is from ourselves or from our supposed support system – if we allow these thoughts to control our journey to becoming successful and succeeding, then we let negativity to win and triumph. What makes negativity a restraint in the mission of becoming successful is that it can be paralyzing so much so that it can turn a dream and vision into a nightmare, an illusion.

Turning negativity into positivity is an obstacle that I had struggled with especially when it came to my mission of succeeding in and becoming something. It is hard when our greatest enemy is the face that is staring us back in the mirror and the that says, you can't be our own voice. We allow these disillusioned beliefs to control every aspect of our lives suddenly, I had used negativity to dominate my perception of self. In a way, this became a constant battle of light and dark because while I knew what I wanted and what I was worthy of, I could not shake these beliefs that I was not meant to be successful or that I would ever amount to much.

Reaching a level of success means not only being able to control and overcome these thoughts and doubt but being able to use it to our advantage productively. I have learned to use the doubt and uncertainty in my life as a means of propelling and thriving for more. Forget the burdens of doubt and embrace the certainty, the certainty that one can amount to more and become a success.

36. FIND WHAT YOU LOVE AND DO IT

> *Success is no accident. It is hard work, perseverance, learning, studying, sacrifice and most of all, love of what you are doing*
>
> – Pele

What differentiates a successful person from an unsuccessful one? They are able to turn their passion into a career if not a career they are able to remember that a life without passion is a life that's dull and boring. While this isn't always the case for most of us – living or being able to make a career of or passion, the principle should be something we hold true or at least attempt to apply in our approach to life. Why? Imagine seeing life as black and white and a mundane, repetitive routine. When you pursue your passion, then you are able to do something you are about, and this is a component of being successful.

When you care, when you show positive feelings and are receptive to your passion – then you can distinguish yourself from everyone else. You stand out from everyone else who is a slave to the system and who work to earn a dollar.

I have learned that being successful does not necessarily mean you are able to make a six-figure pay cheque if anything being successful means that you can wake up day in and day out and know that you are happy. You have lived your life without regrets and without reluctance to ensure you have taken a leap and taken chances. This perceived notion of success equating to wealth is one that society has placed on our understanding of normality but when you look at some of the happiest people, the happiest countries – it is only then that you realize money and success don't correlate. What correlates though is success and happiness.

The results of becoming and achieving success can be complicated but what makes success all the worthier is when you find your passion, your strength – it makes every day afterwards a journey and adventure worth embarking.

37. IF YOU DREAM IT YOU CAN BE IT

The man who has confidence in himself gains the confidence of others

– Hasidic Proverb

What traits make a successful person? Dedication, persistence and opportunist. While some would argue an opportunist is negative, when it comes to becoming and finding our success, an opportunist will take chances and risks. Visualization is a powerful tool and, in a way, if you can dream it, you can achieve it. This can be hard to do when one feels as though the cards are stacked against them – from the lack of support to the lack of confidence, pursuing one's dream can be hard.

What if you can't dream to achieve it?

We are all capable of dreaming – if anything it is almost the one thing that successful and unsuccessful have in common, they dream. The difference between the two is those who genuinely want their dream to become a reality, who want to aspire to more will work tooth and nail and will strive to achieve it.

Those, however, who are not successful, they will continuously dream and just talk about their dreams and never act on it. They will never put the effort in to achieve their goal or to make it a reality but more importantly – they will feel as though the world owes them their dream.

Success is knowing that the world owes us nothing and that to achieve anything more than a normal life requires hard work, dedication and a ream.

38. TAKE ACTION AND MAKE YOUR OWN OPPORTUNITIES

We generate fears while we sit.
We overcome them by action

– Dr. Henry Link

On the journey to becoming a success and finding my potential in this dog-eat-dog world, I have come to learn that opportunities don't always come when we want, and sometimes they'll happen when we take the first step and seize the opportunity. The moment we don't grasp at an opportunity and take a chance that is the moment we allow for failure and not a success. Successful people are successful not because of luck or because they have been given opportunities – they are successful because they chose to seize all and any chances that would and could lead to their growth and development.

We may think that it's hard to know when we are supposed to take life by the horns and go with the flow of things; however, I believe that there is this innate and almost natural instinct where we know what to do and when. It can be hard to describe, if one were to ask someone who is successful in their field, they would at one point of their story say that they just knew, that the cards and stars aligned. In a way, this is what distinguishes a successful person from not. An unsuccessful person will not seize an opportunity – whether it is networking or asking for help, an unsuccessful person will think success is meant to be accomplished alone. One who is successful though – no matter the circumstances, they will seize the opportunity no matter how big, or small, they know that success, it is accomplished with the help of like-minded people.

Take the time, the journey and see it as an array of opportunities that are best enjoyed when we act. Success does not come from inaction and sitting still.

39. DON'T SETTLE ON MEDIOCRITY – GO THE EXTRA MILE

Knowing is not enough; we must apply. Wishing is not enough; we must do

– Johann Wolfgang Von Goethe

Whether it is thinking outside the box, going against the grain or being true to yourself – success comes not out of mediocrity but out of merit and distinction. It happens when we know what it takes to be a success, and then we act and do because if we choose to stay walking the line and not striving for more – that is just not enough. It is not enough to showcase what we are truly capable of achieving but also the potential that can be harnessed when we step out of conformity.

I use to think that just sticking to the path and doing as I was told would lead to my success – everyone else before me seemed to have thrived by doing as I was doing; however, I quickly learned that this was and is not the case. I could follow orders, I could follow the rules, but the truth was, this approach of following regulations and following guidelines was not going to be the way to stick out or be successful. I had to take everything I did to the next level, this means going that extra mile. I worked a little harder, I did everything I could to stick out from the rest of the crowd because I knew that by providing work and showing my abilities made me stand out from the rest. I was paving my way to becoming a success, and I was working towards a goal and dream.

Success is not easy – it doesn't matter whether that success is meant to be a life-changing decision or just making a choice for the present, success comes the moment we step out of our comfort zone, step out of the box, and we put in the hard work. That is success, but more importantly, that is when we know we have separated ourselves from everyone else who seems to think and understand what success is. Be unique, be who you truly are.

40. FAIL ONCE, TRY AGAIN AND LEARN A LESSON

We may encounter many defeats but we must never be defeated

– Maya Angelou

When we strive to become a success in our own right – we often find failing at any step of the way a challenge and sometimes, it can push us to want to give up when we begin to falter or veer off our path. Resilience is a trait of a successful person because it means that when they fail, or when they encounter a problem they are able to pick up the pieces and work towards a solution or an alternative. While 1+1=2, some things in life don't just have one answer – and one of those things is the path to success.

Failing is not a sign of failure, giving up is. Failing, trying again and learning why we failed – that is success, at least a step closer towards it. I am my worst critic, I am also very hard on myself and will see failing as a sign to give up, but over time, when I failed and decided to try something else, I found that failing did not become a failure – it became a lesson. A lesson on how to improve and better myself, but also an experience in what it takes to become a success when everyone else around me also was quitting at the first inkling of failure.

When we have a dream or a goal, and we fail on the way to attaining this – if we indeed are passionate about this dream and goal, we would not walk away so easily. We would fight tooth and nail, but more importantly, we would try and try again. We would take our short-comings and see why did we fail? Why did I not succeed? These are questions that can only be uncovered by trying until we get to where we want to be – until we succeed and we remember all the lessons we learned on our path to becoming a success.

Life teaches us failing is terrible – it is only bad when we allow it to hold us back. Failing can be a sign to be creative, to find your voice and to show yourself what you are capable of.

41. DON'T BE DECEIVED BY SUCCESS – IT CAN MASK FAILURE

You learn more from failure than from success. Don't let it stop you. Failure builds character

– Unknown

One life lesson that I have learned to not only be hard to comprehend but sometimes believe is that success isn't always positive nor is it actually a success. So often we find ourselves thinking that an achievement we have succeeded in is actually a success but the truth of the matter is – they are just obstacles if not distractions to diverge us from attaining true success. This is sometimes hard to accept and think because when we achieve something, that to the naked eye is a success, a win we take it for what it is – a victory.

The difference though when it comes to knowing what is a failure masked by success and when an accomplishment is, in fact, an achievement, lies in our ability to understand what is our dream, our goal and what do we hope to achieve. If we are content with all the little victories then in a way, failures can be accepted as successes – but then our real potential isn't fully achieved.

Knowing our standards, our expectations and what it is we want to accomplish and where our top of the ladder is – that is when we know a success is not a failure and a failure is not a success.

42. TAKE THE FIRST STEP TOWARDS SUCCESS

A no.2 pencil and a dream can take you anywhere

– Joyce Meyer

Where does the journey to becoming a success begin? With a pen and paper, or pencil if you like to play it carefully and be able to make erase mistakes. When I was younger I dreamt of becoming an astronaut and then a lawyer – as I got older, I began to focus on a realistic approach to pursuing my passion but also setting the motions to becoming a success. Once you write out what it is you hope to pursue and turn into a reality – these achievements, no matter how big or small become the foundation and platform for reaching the top of the ladder.

Visualizing and seeing what it is we want and hope to achieve not only makes it real but it helps to take that first step towards that path of becoming successful. I am a visual person, I write everything down – from notes to reminders to what I hope to accomplish, I write things down because seeing it on paper makes it feel as though we are one step closer to achieving the goal we set out for ourselves. When we write, when we create a plan of what we want and hope to accomplish we demonstrate why we are bound to be a success. We understand that being successful is not easy, nor does it just happen walking down a street – it happens with planning, prepping and execution.

If one can dream it and then act on it – they already have a leg up on the competition.

43. LITTLE CAN BE MORE

*It is always the simple that
produces the marvelous*

– Amelia Barr

There is a reason that when it comes to fashion, the little black dress or the white tee can be seen as making a statement and yet it is as minimal as one can get when it comes to fashion. Success can be correlated to this analogy because sometimes it is the little things we do that speak wonders. It is important though that one not confuse the simple acts as doing nothing or sticking to the status-quo – this is not the case. It is knowing when the small acts – whether they be in the decision, the choices or how we perceive what success is, sometimes less is more.

When we look at life and all that it has to offer – there is a reason for the saying of less is more because for the most part we are inundated with messages of more is better. From how we should live our life – the cars we drive, the house we live in but also how we should live. We are pressured to live a lifestyle of more and more and the only way of attaining this is by doing more; however, while society may push these values on us it does not equate or transfer into becoming a success. When we strive to become successful in life, we think that this is the approach to take – be loud, be proud and stick out. This may work in some aspects of becoming a success; however, consistency and dedication isn't about who is the loudest and most out there it is about consistency.

To be a success one must know themselves but more importantly, they must understand and see that our actions don't need to be extreme if anything they need to be true to yourself and true to your goal and dream. By living a life of meaningful actions only then is true and worthy success achieved.

44. SUCCESS COMES FROM THOSE WHO TAKE TIME TO LISTEN

*Most of the successful people
I've known are the ones who do
more listening than talking*

– Bernard Baruch

Did you know that one of the most underestimated skills of someone who is successful is listening? When we take the time to listen rather than talk – some benefits show leadership but also the traits of a successful person. I have learned from personal experience that silence can be more potent than words spoken. When I look back at my some of my shortcomings, a pattern that makes itself very apparent was my inability to listen before speaking.

Why was this a shortcoming? Why was not just defending myself and showing why I was right or better not the solution? Simple – leaders listen, successful people listen and unsuccessful people talk. They talk, and they disregard discussion. When someone is successful – they listen to learn, to understand and to be informed. Showing our ability to listen and be a good and active listener means building and

45. BE OPEN TO IDEAS, DIVERSITY AND ADVERSITY

Without an open-minded mind, you can never be a great success

– Martha Stewart

How one handles adversity, diversity and new ideas can separate those from who are successful and those who are not because someone who is successful sees the value in thinking outside the box. An unsuccessful person would not be open to new and out of the box ideas, they would disregard diversity and struggle with adversity. When someone is successful, they know that those who also think and see the world the same way as they understand the value of non-traditional approaches. Going against the grain, knowing one's strengths and knowing that being successful is not about being like everyone else is what distinguish the successful from unsuccessful.

Striving for success means knowing that adversity is the new traditional and indeed reaching one's potential means being open-minded because the greatest minds, inventors, entrepreneurs were the ones who saw the world for more than what's on the surface. Successful people know that the world is multi-dimensional and just as it is this, I have learned that success can only be achieved by embracing this notion. Embrace change, embrace diversity and embrace adversity because it is only then that we can reach our potential, our potential for success.

46. TRUST YOUR GUT AND YOUR INSTINCT

Have the courage to follow your heart and intuition. They somehow know what you truly want to becoming

– Steve Jobs

There is a saying where, when you know, you just know. In a way that is why we have that fight or flight response and why sometimes we are able to decide without truly understanding why we do what we do or why we react a certain way. When it comes to wanting to be successful, we will find that on the journey to the top we will see times our instincts automatically kick in. In a way, we sometimes think we know what we want better than anyone else – this stands true unless we actually don't know ourselves. When we hold back when we work towards someone else is dream – then we actually don't know ourselves.

When we know what it is we want to achieve, what we want and we trust ourselves – we are able to listen to our heart, and what it is we are being guided to. Entrepreneurs, businessmen, and those who are successful will trust their instinct and make decisions they know are right for them. The battle though is when we don't dare to listen to our gut or believe ourselves to make the right choice. The risks, the chances and opportunities that present themselves and we have to decide – we will always know the answer and what to pick, it is just a matter of trusting we make the right one.

47. BE SUCCESSFUL WITH HUMILITY

There are two rules for success:
1. Never tell everything you know.

– Roger H. Lincoln

In a way some would say I am being a hypocrite by saying that we should strive to be successful and humble altogether; however, a successful person would argue this is what they do and why they are successful. There is a multi-million if not billion-dollar industry on self-help books and how to succeed; therefore, it seems almost ironic that one would say the secret to success is not saying anything. The truth is, success is attained not by a single path but by individual choices and decisions.

Success through humility is not just about boasting, but it is also about understanding that only because we succeeded does not mean our success can be replicated by another – let alone can we dictate to others how to also be successful. Being successful, even if we intend to share insight on how we reached the top and to be helpful can sometimes actually make things worse, it can discourage someone from thinking they can achieve more.

I have achieved my personal on a level of success – and though some would say this book and my tips contradict this approach; however, there is this gray area where sharing stories of becoming successful and tips are not dictating how one should be when growing successful.

48. COMPETE WITH YOURSELF AND GROW

Life does not require that we be the best, only that we try our best

– H. Jackson Brown Jr.

When it comes to climbing the ladder to success, we often compare ourselves to everyone else around us. We see what others are doing, and we see how we can compete and how we can one-up everyone; however, who we should be competing with is no one but ourselves. We should always strive to better ourselves and no one else because when we compare our accomplishments, then we are not succeeding to be better but we are succeeding for everyone else. The standards that one person has for what is success to them is not the same as what another sees as success.

Becoming successful is a multitude of factors, and one of those factors is trying, trying and doing their best. Competition not only motivates but it aids in our pursuit of becoming a better version of ourselves but also competition separates those who enjoy a challenge and aspire to more. The ladder to the top is exclusive for a reason, and that is because those who make it there compete with no one but themselves. They create milestone after milestone and never stop trying and being better. This is a level of success and growth that distinguishes the successful from unsuccessful.

49. SUCCEED TO LEAD AND BE REMEMBERED

Don't chase people. Be an example. Attract them. Work hard and be yourself. The people who belong in your life will come and find you and stay. Just do you thing.

- Unknown

As a teenager, one of the things I always wondered about was what kind of legacy and reputation would people remember about me when I went on to university. As an adult, this is something I think about still, about whether or not my reputation and accomplishments would make me memorable or if I would be like everyone else – forgettable.

Once I found my groove and embraced both my failures and achievements, I realized that my legacy, reputation would be remembered by those who mattered and those who did not, they did not matter in the grand scheme of my life. Successful people, they compete with themselves and ignore everyone else around them because they know what they want in life. Not only do they know what they want in life but they know that those who are successful don't boast or succeed to make others happy. They understand that being successful and their achievements aren't meant for anyone else but for them.

Strive to know that what we do and the energy we put into the universe will be recognized by those who appreciate and value the hard work and effort. The example we become, and the life we lead will be one that those who want to be successful as well will feel inspired and motivated by.

50. NEVER STOP LEARNING AND NEVER STOP TRYING

Success is not final, failure is not fatal: it is the courage to continue that counts

- Unknown

What does one do when we they've reached the top of the ladder of success? They continue onwards, and they find new ways of achieving a new level of success. I use to think that once I made one milestone and accomplishment, that was it; however, I realized later on that there was so much more that I wanted to accomplish. The top 1% of the ladder that houses those successful and inspirational people don't sit still and let others try to join the club – they aspire to be more and try to outdo themselves.

Failure or success, the courage to keep going is what separates those who are meant to be successful and those who are not. The moment we let failure, or we let that first million dollars hold us back from achieving another million – that is neither success nor failure, it is an illusion of progress. Complacency on the journey to succeeding is sometimes an easier route to take, and while this may be the case the question we have to ask ourselves is – are we happy? Have we truly succeeded?

Climb that ladder to succeed and never stop learning or trying because the moment we do, then we have lost sight of our dreams, hopes and goals.

OTHER HELPFUL RESOURCES

11 Secrets to Becoming Rich, Successful and Happy
https://www.inc.com/jeff-haden/11-secrets-to-becoming-rich-successful-and-happy.html

6 Things You Should Quit Doing To Become Successful
https://www.forbes.com/sites/glassheel/2013/10/01/6-things-you-should-quit-to-be-more-successful/#75c343c4423d

10 Tips to Achieve Anything You Want
https://www.success.com/10-tips-to-achieve-anything-you-want-in-life/

50 Things to Know

READ OTHER 50 THINGS TO KNOW BOOKS

50 Things to Know to Get Things Done Fast: Easy Tips for Success

50 Things to Know About Going Green: Simple Changes to Start Today

50 Things to Know to Live a Happy Life Series

50 Things to Know to Organize Your Life: A Quick Start Guide to Declutter, Organize, and Live Simply

50 Things to Know About Being a Minimalist: Downsize, Organize, and Live Your Life

50 Things to Know About Speed Cleaning: How to Tidy Your Home in Minutes

50 Things to Know About Choosing the Right Path in Life

50 Things to Know to Get Rid of Clutter in Your Life: Evaluate, Purge, and Enjoy Living

50 Things to Know About Journal Writing: Exploring Your Innermost Thoughts & Feelings

50 Things to Know

Website: 50thingstoknow.com

Facebook: facebook.com/50thingstoknow

Pinterest: pinterest.com/lbrennec

YouTube: youtube.com/user/50ThingsToKnow

Twitter: twitter.com/50ttk

Mailing List: Join the 50 Things to Know Mailing List to Learn About New Releases

50 Things to Know

Please leave your honest review of this book on Amazon and Goodreads. We appreciate your positive and constructive feedback. Thank you.

www.ingramcontent.com/pod-product-compliance
Lightning Source LLC
Chambersburg PA
CBHW030723220526
45463CB00005B/2150